MAY 2 3 2017

D1360060

NUESTRAS COMUNIDADES
—
AMERICAN COMMUNITIES

Vivimos en el campo

—

We Live in the Country

Mary Austen

Traducido por Esther Sarfatti

PowerKiDS press.

New York

Published in 2016 by The Rosen Publishing Group, Inc.
29 East 21st Street, New York, NY 10010

Copyright © 2016 by The Rosen Publishing Group, Inc.

All rights reserved. No part of this book may be reproduced in any form without permission in writing from the publisher, except by a reviewer.

First Edition

· Editor: Katie Kawa
Book Design: Reann Nye
Traducido por: Esther Sarfatti

Photo Credits: Cover, pp. 3–24 (background texture) Evgeny Karandaev/Shutterstock.com; cover Sahani Photography/Shutterstock.com; p. 5 Kzenon/Shutterstock.com; p. 6 cdrin/Shutterstock.com; p. 9 (country) Francesco Ferrarini/Shutterstock.com; p. 9 (city) Manamana/Shutterstock.com; p. 10 WDG Photo/Shutterstock.com; p. 13 nata-lunata/Shutterstock.com; pp. 14, 24 (ranch) MaxyM/ Shutterstock.com; p. 17 Ozerov Alexander/Shutterstock.com; p. 18 mlorenz/Shutterstock.com; pp. 21, 24 (field mouse) davemhuntphotography/Shutterstock.com; p. 22 Jon Bilous/Shutterstock.com.

Cataloging-in-Publication Data

Austen, Mary.
We live in the country = Vivimos en el campo / by Mary Austen.
p. cm. — (American communities = Nuestras comunidades)
Parallel title: Nuestras comunidades.
In English and Spanish.
Includes index.
ISBN 978-1-5081-4738-1 (library binding)
1. Country life — Juvenile literature. I. Austen, Mary. II. Title.
QH48.A97 2016
578.7—d23

Manufactured in the United States of America

CPSIA Compliance Information: Batch #BW16PK: For Further Information contact Rosen Publishing, New York, New York at 1-800-237-9932

Contenido
Contents

El campo es un lugar
hermoso para vivir.

The country is a beautiful
place to live.

3 0053 01243 7086

5

Al campo también se le puede llamar comunidad rural.

The country is also known as a rural community.

En el campo vive menos gente que en la ciudad. También hay menos casas y edificios.

There are fewer people living in the country than in a city. There are fewer homes and other buildings, too.

campo
country

ciudad
city

9

Por lo general, las casas y otros edificios están alejados unos de otros. ¡Vivimos lejos de nuestros vecinos!

Homes and other buildings in the country are often far from one another. We live far from our neighbors!

11

Algunas personas que viven en el campo trabajan en la ciudad. Tienen que hacer un largo viaje para ir a trabajar todos los días.

Some people who live in the country work in the city.
They drive a long way to work each day.

13

Algunas personas que viven en el campo trabajan en **ranchos**. Un rancho es una granja grande donde viven vacas y caballos.

Some people who live in the country work on **ranches**. A ranch is a big farm where cows and horses live.

El campo es un lugar ideal
para los caballos.
¡Tienen mucho espacio
para correr!

The country is a great place
for horses to live. They have a
lot of room to run!

Vemos muchos animales salvajes en el campo. ¡Los búhos vuelan en el cielo campestre!

We see many wild animals in the country. Owls fly in the country sky!

Los ratones de campo viven en los campos abiertos. Los podemos ver durante un paseo por la finca.

Field mice live in the open fields of the country. We see them when we walk around our land.

21